Conversations with Super-centenarian Violet Mosse-Brown

BY VALOMIA MOSS-WEIR

VIOLET HENRIETTA MOSSE-BROWN

Published by
WTL International
930 North Park Drive
P.O. Box 33049
Brampton, Ontario
L6S 6A7 Canada
www.wtlipublishing.com

978-1-778310-02-7

Printed in the U.S.A.

ACKNOWLEDGEMENTS

ACKNOWLEDGEMENTS

Writing a book about the story of a loved one is a surreal process. I'm indebted to my daughters Kareen Weir and Krystal Weir as well as my siblings and nephew Denver Bloomfield, for the encouragement I received to make this book a reality.

I am also grateful to my friend Mary Bailey and Aisha Hammah, my publisher, for their editorial help, keen insight, and ongoing support in bringing my aunt's story to life. It is because of their collective efforts and encouragement that I have a legacy to pass on not just to my family but to the world at large.

I extend my appreciation to everyone on my publishing team.

Thanks to the Guinness World Records. I gratefully acknowledge permission to use

Guinness World Records copyrighted material in this publication.

Finally, a huge thank you to Violet Mosse-Brown (R.I.P.) who shared her gift of time and history with me. We shared hours and hours of recorded conversations during which she educated me about my background, among other things. When I want to be inspired, I often listen to her voice on tape and reminisce on the precious moments we had. Without her candid accounts and the valuable time she shared with me, this book would not have been possible.

TABLE OF CONTENTS

INTRODUCTION

VIOLET HENRIETTA MOSSE-BROWN

INTRODUCTION

Violet Brown, formerly Violet Mosse, born on March 10, 1900, was the first verified super-centenarian from Jamaica and the oldest verified Jamaican person. She was born when Jamaica was part of the British Empire. She was one of the last persons known to have been born in the 19th century and a former subject of Queen Victoria.

In 2014, the Gerontology Research Group recognized March 10, 1900 as her birth date. Previously, there were uncertainties surrounding her birth date. For many years she celebrated it on March 15.

Violet was the second of four children born to John Gordon Mosse, a sugar boiler and Elizabeth Riley, a domestic helper.

Her other siblings who all predeceased her were Wellesley, Christobel and William, my father.

Violet survived two world wars. She was born before the first plane and motor car got to Jamaica. Violet had a family history of longevity. She lived in a comfortable family environment, had been a hard worker and possessed well-preserved psychological and cognitive abilities. She was free from certain risk factors such as hypertension and high cholesterol and she had always followed a balanced diet, based on natural foods. This book will give you a glimpse of the life of this phenomenal woman.

FAMILY BACKGROUND

VIOLET HENRIETTA MOSSE-BROWN

FAMILY BACKGROUND

Violet's mother, Elizabeth Mosse, was from the district of Duanvale, Trelawny in Jamaica but her father, John Gordon Mosse of the McIntosh family, was from Daniel Town and Spicy Hill in the same parish.

Violet did not know her father's mother, but she knew her mother's family members well. Some of her family members are from Dry Hill and Refuge in Trelawny. Although Violet's mother was from Duanvale, she grew up in Falmouth, the parish capital, with her stepmother. Violet surmised that there was probably where her parents met and fell in love. Her grandmother was Jane Eve Clarke, and her grandfather was Robert Ruffin Riley. She didn't know them but recalled they were born a little after slavery had ended.

VIOLET HENRIETTA MOSSE-BROWN

REFLECTIONS

VIOLET HENRIETTA MOSSE-BROWN

REFLECTIONS

As a dear niece who grew up next door, I could say Violet's property was my old stomping ground. Many memories are etched in my mind of the wonderful moments we shared. I remember her storytelling fondly. I was consumed by her stories of the Maccabee Bible. This version was an extension of Bible. Her favourite book of the Maccabees was Tobit. I was lost in the story about how Tobit was blinded by the warm dung of sparrows and his family descended into poverty due to disobeying Jewish law. Another memory that stands out is how much of a disciplinarian Aunt V was. When we visited, her role was that of monitoring us while we played. There was an incident where one of my cousins provoked me to the point where I punched him in the soft spot between his ribs and out of nowhere Aunt V shouted, "Lord, God! What happen to him?" She then quickly mixed some sugar and water and gave it to him and had us sitting quietly afterwards.

As a child, I remember Aunt V was the first one on our street to have some of the amenities we, as well as the community at large, didn't have at the time. Aunt V had a kerosine oil refrigerator. It was a novelty, and I was excited to see how it functioned. We were able to get ice and we loved it especially on Sundays to cool the prized carrot juice we had, made with beet and Dragon Stout, then sweetened with condensed milk. She also sold ice made in various containers as well as large polythene bags to community folk who lived in close vicinity.

Aunt V had a black-and-white Westing-house television set. I vividly remember sitting on her rug watching American shows like *Bonanza*, *Skippy* the *Bush Kangaroo*, *The Flying Nun* and *Lassie*, to name a few. My sister, my nephews and I were always welcome as long as we followed her strict ground rules which included removing our shoes and remaining quiet.

Aunt V's Reed organ, Duanvale, Trelawny

Violet had an old Reed organ that was her pride and joy and one of her favourite songs to play was "Beautiful Dreamer." On occasion, her organ was re-tuned by a faithful community friend who checked the billows and keys as well as adjusted the buttons. I would sit and listen to the choristers who would visit her home on a Thursday to practice the hymns for the upcoming Sunday service.

It was always a joy to run next door to see Violet. Aunt V had a wealth of information and never hesitated to share stories about her life experiences and about the district of Duanvale. On several occasions, the opportunity presented itself for me to quiz her on her family background, childhood days, work, fashion, and contribution to the community. On one of my trips to the district, a month before her passing, I seized the moment to interview Aunt V who had me spellbound with stories that spanned more than a century.

A picture of Aunt V and me taken on her last Mother's Day at age 117 in May of 2017, hours after the Thanksgiving service for her son Harland Fairweather, Duanvale, Trelawny

Violet began with a historical briefing on my grandparents John and Elizabeth Mosse. She couldn't recall where their pictures were but recollected that her mother Elizabeth Mosse was a hard worker whose primary occupation was a domestic helper up until her death in 1966.

Elizabeth was not a sharp dresser, as her days were more ancient, but her old style of dressing became what Violet knew. Aunt V recounted going to church one Sunday and that she was going to "tidy" (get ready). When she put on her undergarments, there were two dresses on the bed, so she turned to her mother and said she didn't know which of the dresses to wear. The sharp retort was, "Daughter, if you can't find none, go naked." There was robust laughter after which she confessed that when she was young, she was very vain. I smiled when she said this, as I distinctly remembered her being well-dressed, heading to church in fancy dresses with her broad-brimmed hats, stiletto heels and pearls.

I always wondered where she got her elegant outfits from. She said all the things she wore came from a firm abroad called Oxendale and Leonard's. This was the United Kingdom's leading direct home shopping company which was founded in 1875 and operated several catalogue brands. Oxendale and Leonard's offered a huge selection of clothing and other products for all ages and sizes. The company was the first to utilize the United Kingdom's parcel post service to send products directly to its customers.

Violet explained with pride how she purchased her products, "There was a catalogue and whatever I liked I marked them off and sent them off. The goods were sent to me later." The items, ranging from shoes of all colours to dresses to pants for men, women and children, were mailed and picked up at the local post office. She was definitely a trendsetter and a fashionista.

Duanvale Post Office, Duanevale, Trelawny

EARLY YEARS

VIOLET HENRIETTA MOSSE-BROWN

EARLY YEARS

Violet attended school at the Methodist Church where her classes were conducted at the time. It was otherwise called "Tup a Week" in the district. The parents paid a penny and ha'penny to school their children. Aunt V attended "Tup a Week" until she was seven years old. In later years, due to vandalism to the church windows, children were removed to what is now the Duanvale Elementary School which is situated on the church compound.

While at "Tup a Week," the first car that came to Jamaica passed through the district. The teacher took the children outside and allowed them to stand on the bank to see it. Aunt V, upon reflecting said, "It was a little red car and the horn said 'puppup' so that was the name we gave to the car."

Duanvale Elementary School, Duanvale, Trelawny

Aunt V then transferred to the "Big School" where she spent seven more years totalling fourteen years of schooling. Violet had two teachers: at "Tup a Week" her teacher was Richard Small, and her teacher at the "Big School" was Luther Welsh.

Aunt V had to complete first to sixth class before leaving Big School (now

Duanvale Primary School). She complained of having a rough time in Big School because the teacher was very "strict and cruel." Violet recalled that the teacher would beat them hard when they did not meet his expectations. The beatings would leave welts.

At this juncture I was intrigued as to why the students were harshly punished. In asking for an example Aunt V replied, "When we got dictations, we had to know our punctuation marks. We had to know where to put the colons, semicolons, commas, dashes, question marks and full stops." She stated that the books were very difficult.

Aunt V did lots of poems in school. One she recounted was "The Sailor's Wife." She recited a small part to me:

"I've a letter from thy sire, baby mine, baby mine.
I can read and never tire, baby mine.
He's sailing o'er the sea. He's coming back to thee. He's coming home to me, baby mine."

Another poem she said she had to learn was "The Vision of Belshazzar." It was the last poem she learned at school. She claimed it was long and tiresome. She loved "Love Lightens Labour." She asked if I understood what the poem meant and started to recite it:

"A good wife rose from her bed and thought of a nervous dread, of piles of clothes to be washed, children to be sent away to school, the farmers to feed, the

animals to be taken care of, milk
to be skimmed and churned, and
all have to be done on this one
day..."

She explained that it was about a woman who had been a maid and who had no children or any man, so whenever she got up in the mornings, she did whatever she could. She complained about all the hard work she had to do. At long last she met a man who loved her, kissed her when he'd leave for work and told her to do just what she could. When he got home, he would ask if she managed to do all her work for the day. He would hug her and say:

"Tis so sweet to labour for those
we love, it's not strange if maids
will wed. If maidens know what
good wives know, they would not
be in any haste to wed."

She then added that the subject of the lesson is "love lightens labour." She stated, "I never understood that lesson until I became a woman with children. That was when I found out what that meant." Her interpretation of the poem was, "No matter how hard the work is, and you have your husband, if both of you love each other, the work will become light."

Duanvale Primary School, Duanvale, Trelawny

Violet and siblings Wellesley, Christobel and William played simple games such as "lick and run," which we now call "tag." Aunt V remembered one day she and Wellesley had a little fuss. He hit her and she started to cry. She went inside the house and her mother asked what was wrong. She reported that her brother had hit her. Her mother called them both, told them to stand in front of her and said, "Repeat after me":

"Let dogs delight to bark and bite for 'tis their nature to. Let bears and lions growl and fight for 'tis their nature to."

Then turning to them she said,

"But children you should never let such angry passion rise. Your

little hands were never made to
tear each other's eyes."

She then placed them in the corner
for a while before sending them back
outside to play with a warning not to hit
anymore.

They grew up with a lot of proverbs or
wise sayings, two of which were, "A wink
at the old horse is better than the whip,"
and "Show me your company, tells me who
you are."

Aunt V and her siblings accompanied
their mother to Sunday School at nine
o'clock before the eleven o'clock service
every Sunday. They rehearsed the 23rd
Psalm as well as other passages of
scripture.

Aunt V remarked that they never grew
up like this present generation. They had

to walk four miles to Sherwood, a neighbouring community by the river, to get water, and return before getting ready for school. She told me of an early morning when she got her container and walked to get water. "I hurried to Sherwood, waited in line to get my bucket filled, then skillfully and carefully walked back home. Upon reaching the gate, I stubbed my toe and the bucket fell, spilling all of the water. I was so overwhelmed with sadness, and I cried uncontrollably to the point where my mother too was tearful." I felt heartbroken when she recalled this incident just thinking of the distance she had walked both ways, how tired she must have been and then having to prepare to get to school. Aunt V couldn't remember when Duanvale got water and electricity. After completing Big School, Aunt V remained at home and did domestic work with her mother, as there were no high schools.

WORKING YEARS

VIOLET HENRIETTA MOSSE-BROWN

WORKING YEARS

Aunt V worked at Florence Hall in Trelawny for five shillings a week. She said, "It was like a boarding school where I learned to do many, many things, including roasting a pig." This was done especially in the months of August and December at Christmastime. She stressed that one had to know what kind of pig to roast. One could not roast a boar pig which is a male pig but a shoat pig which is a "sucker," a pig between birth and weaning. In her own words, she said the reason why a boar pig could not be roasted is:

"The boar pig got two seed behind him, and you can't get anywhere to cut but the woman pig has a vagina where you can push your hand right up and draw out the pig belly (intestines)."

She disclosed this with a robust laugh. At this point I was on the verge of tears, unable to control my laughter. She further explained the process, "The head remained but the feet were cut off, the ears were split and cleaned, and the eyeballs removed. The inside of the pig was cleaned and set aside. A big pudding pan was used to combine the stuffing, mainly pepper, onions and thyme, which was placed inside the pig before sewing it up and roasting it. The roasted pig was then placed on a tin sheet and set on the table. The table was set with carving knives and forks and persons cut pieces they wanted. The remaining portion was cut up for friends and eaten at a later time." Violet however did not eat pork even though she could do such a great job of roasting it. She made me privy to her reason for not eating pork and it was so hilarious. We both laughed so hard, I could hardly maintain my composure but of course some things we will take to the grave.

It was while Aunt V was at Florence Hall that the first airplane passed over Jamaica. It passed on a Saturday she recalled. "It was a little white plane with some white streaks behind it. People said it was a jet." She never saw it, but many people came out to see it. They said that a fish flew out of the sea into the sky. They said that it was a fish because of its shape.

After leaving Florence Hall, Aunt V went to Falmouth for a few years to work with the Delgado family. She went there as a butleress. She waited around the table, but she never did any washing or cooking. Every morning she would get ready in her navy-blue dress, white apron, white cap, and black shoes.

Violet worked to make a living for her

family juggling jobs as a one-time dressmaker, domestic helper, shopkeeper, and farmer. Violet started working as a cane farmer before meeting her husband. She met and married Augustus Gaynor Brown who was two years younger than her and who also resided in Duanvale. The dates of their meeting and marriage eluded her. According to her, "Hard work removed some of the information." They both combined their efforts, cultivating corn, coffee and cane.

As a cane farmer, Violet alongside her husband Augustus, was one of the major players. She had cane fields and workers who she employed to cultivate and harvest the cane. This was then trucked to the Long Pond Sugar Factory in Clark's Town Trelawny for processing.

Violet had awesome culinary skills. She was a great cook who was passionate about food and cooking. She could cook ground provisions in only plain water with a piece of pork skin and made it so delectable. I had the opportunity to observe her and to consume several scrumptious meals in her kitchen.

In addition to farming, Violet operated a bread shop across from the community post office. She reminisced that her shop was full on Tuesdays and Fridays with children who came to get bulla cakes. These are Jamaican cakes made with flour, sugar, and molasses, spiced with nutmeg and ginger. They are great with avocado or cheese. Violet recounted that many of those students visited her later on in life to express their gratitude to her for the kindness shown to them as children.

Violet went on to say, "No book can

hold my stories, but I thank God for all the good that I have done; as the little book says, 'Do all the good you can in all the ways you can to all the people you can just as long as you can.' Thank God for all I've done. I'm getting every pay now. I have to ask myself, 'Is it I'?"

Augustus, who we called "Mass Guss," went to his cane field one early morning in August of 1978 to tend to his crops. After having lunch with the other workers, he joked around with them and rested for a moment before resuming work. "Mass Guss" took a while to rejoin his work team and appeared to be napping. Upon closer inspection the co-workers realized that he had died with his cutlass in his hand. He was a hard cultivator who did all he could to make a living.

THE LEGACY

VIOLET HENRIETTA MOSSE-BROWN

THE LEGACY

Violet's parents informed her that they had been conducting prayer meetings at a location undisclosed to her, however they had asked for a plot of land from one Mr. Shirley to build a church. It was granted but they had no money to start building. Her parents approached a man named Mr. Tritt for a donation to begin construction. When the church was built, it was called Trittonville Baptist Church. This was the first church in the district of Duanvale.

Trittonville Baptist Church, Duanvale, Trelawny

Trittonville Baptist Church was the only church in the entire district until a man named Mr. Fraser gave a piece of land to build another church. When it was completed, it was called Fraserville Methodist Church.

Fraserville Methodist Church, Duanvale, Trelawny

The land given was a huge piece, stretching from Palmer's Crescent, going up to Shirley Hill. There wasn't enough money to expand the church, so a piece of the land was taken and sold to the parochial authority to bury persons. It is now the Duanvale Cemetery. Violet assisted her husband with recording the deaths in the community, as well as distributing of the burial plots and maintaining the grounds.

Duanvale Cemetery, Duanvale, Trelawny

Violet said that Duanvale developed little by little like a big pond:

"If you pick up a gravel and throw it into the pond, stand there and watch it. You will see like a little ring, and it never stops until it is all burst out. That is Duanvale. It was a little place, but the people then come in and build around until it is this big."

Some of the other areas of development were the health centre and the community centre where community events were hosted, and persons learned to make craft items as well as develop culinary skills.

Duanvale Health Centre, Duanvale, Trelawny

Duanvale Community Centre, Duanvale, Trelawny

Violet was baptized when she was thirteen years old by Reverend A. G. Eccleston. The scripture passage given at her reception was Psalm 119, verse 133, "Order my steps in Thy word, let no sin have no dominion over me." She confessed to falling at times, but she was always holding on to God. She said, "God helped me to be everything in the Baptist Church from organist to class leader to helper, assisting with the reroofing of the church." She was also a deaconess, choir director, hospitality coordinator, counselor, church secretary, member of the Women's Federation and the Christian Endeavour and member of the Officer's Board. Violet served with distinction and pride in all areas that were assigned to her. She was a woman of vision, fueled by her deep faith in God. She was one of the pioneers who was instrumental in having the addition done to the eastern section of the chapel which brought much joy and comfort to the ministers. She had been a member of the church for over 100 years.

A monument was erected in honour of Violet's mother, Elizabeth Mosse, for the building of the church.

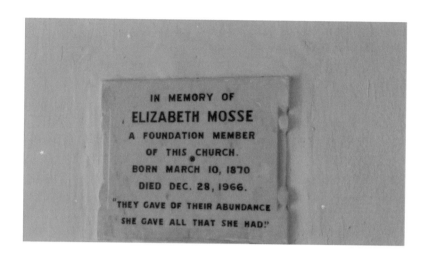

A wall placard in memory of Violet's mother at Trittonville Baptist Church, Duanvale, Trelawny

Violet believed God has a plan for every man and woman. She said she cried and felt lonely sometimes because her friends and relatives had predeceased her, but she had God as her companion. She felt good reflecting on her school days and her church life. Violet had no medical complaints, just the inability to hear well which did not affect her much. She attributed her long life to hard work and good food. In her own words, "When people ask what me eat and drink to live so long, I tell them I eat everything except pork and chicken. I don't drink rum and them things." Coconut sauce with fish is something else she attributed to her long life. The coconut sauce is made with freshly squeezed coconut milk boiled with escallion, salt, pimento seeds, onion, butter, pepper, and thyme. The fish is added after to simmer for a few minutes. Violet loved sugar cane and enjoyed eating it without the use of dentures as she had sturdy teeth.

Violet read her Daily Bread devotional each day flawlessly without the assistance of eyeglasses. She also made reference to an extract from the Ten Commandments, "Honour your mother and father so your days may be long on the earth," as another reason for a long and fruitful life. She thanked God for sparing her life and enabling her to obtain the ripe age of 117 years by ending with this quote: "A thousand ages in Thy sight is like an evening gone, short as the watch that ends the night before the rising sun." She expressed that she wanted to read the Bible from cover to cover but that desire was not realized. She was only able to complete the first five books.

Violet remembered as a young girl having to use bottles to make lamps at night because she had no light. She could not afford to be outdoors at nightfall, so she had to complete her chores early. Young people of today, she believed, have it easy with piped water, taxis and buses at their convenience. She recalled, "When I was younger, it was hard for me and it sometimes brings me to tears upon reflection."

Violet had one daughter with Augustus. She had six children in total. Her first child was thought to be the oldest person to have lived with a living parent prior to her death.

Violet being awarded her certificate of recognition from Guinness World Records, Duanvale, Trelawny. Courtesy of guinnessworldrecords.com (Ott, 2017)

Violet is featured in the **Guinness World Records 2018** book. She was presented with her certificate at her home in Duanvale, Trelawny, Jamaica on September 3, 2017 by Guinness World

Records' Director of Latin America Carlos Martinez. Carlos Martinez had these wonderful words to say about Violet: "It was truly an honour to present Ms. Violet Brown with her Guinness World Records certificate for being the oldest person living, as she put it, 'in the entire world'." He further went on to say, "Not every day does one have the opportunity to share some time with the person who has been on this planet the longest" (Ott, 2017).

Violet looking at herself in a Guinness Book of World Records, Duanvale, Trelawny. Courtesy of guinnessworldrecords.com (Ott, 2017)

Sadly, just days after the presentation, Violet died peacefully after a brief illness on September 15, 2017. A host of family, friends, and well-wishers from all across Jamaica and other parts of the world gathered on October 7 at the Trittonville Baptist Church to celebrate her life. Her body was donated to the University of the West Indies (UWI) for scientific research. On September 15, 2021, the fourth anniversary of Violet's passing, a storyboard which was erected by the Ministry of Culture, Gender, Entertainment and Sport and the Trelawny Municipal Corporation was unveiled at her home. A life-sized bust was completed by Jamaican sculptor Pamrie Dwyer, for permanent display in the district of Duanvale.

CONCLUSION

VIOLET HENRIETTA MOSSE-BROWN

CONCLUSION

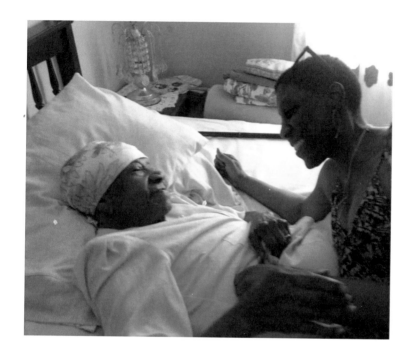

Aunt V and I sharing a tender moment on my visit to Duanvale in May 2017 for her son's funeral, Duanvale, Trelawny

Violet Mosse-Brown has made an impact on her community, Jamaica at large and numerous persons with whom she has crossed paths. As her niece, she has left valuable memories with me such as her warmth and humour that brightened my days. She loved to laugh; there was never a dull moment around her, the consummate storyteller and historian. Some values and virtues learned from her are hard work, devotion to duty, her wisdom, her healthy eating regimen, offering hospitality to others, and the magnificence of life with grace and fortitude. Aunt V has left me life-lasting memories which I will always treasure.

Life is richer because we shared your moment. Still missed, still loved and cherished.

REFERENCES

Kristen Ott. (2017). *World's oldest person Violet Moss-Brown from Jamaica dies age 117.* www.guinnessworldrecords.com. Taken from: https://www.guinnessworldrecords.com/

In Guinness World Records Limited. (2017). *Guinness world records 2018.*